Thundering Niagara

Falling in love with the power and wonder of Niagara Falls, USA

by Mark Donnelly, Ph.D.

RPSS Publishing • Buffalo, New York
www.rpsspublishing.com

Thundering Niagara - Falling in love with the power and wonder of Niagara Falls, USA
Hardcover - 978-1-956688-48-1
Perfect Bound - 978-1-956688-49-8

RPSS Publishing - Buffalo, NY 14223
publisher@rockpapersafetyscissors.com

First Edition

25 24 23 22 21 6 5 4 3 2 1

Printed in the United States of America

"By what mysterious power is it that millions and millions, are drawn from all parts of the world?"

A. Lincoln & family
July 25th 1857

He also pondered:
"The thing that struck me most forcibly when I saw the Falls was, where in the world did all that water come from?"

(Abraham Lincoln's signature is from the Cataract House Hotel guest book - July 25, 1857)

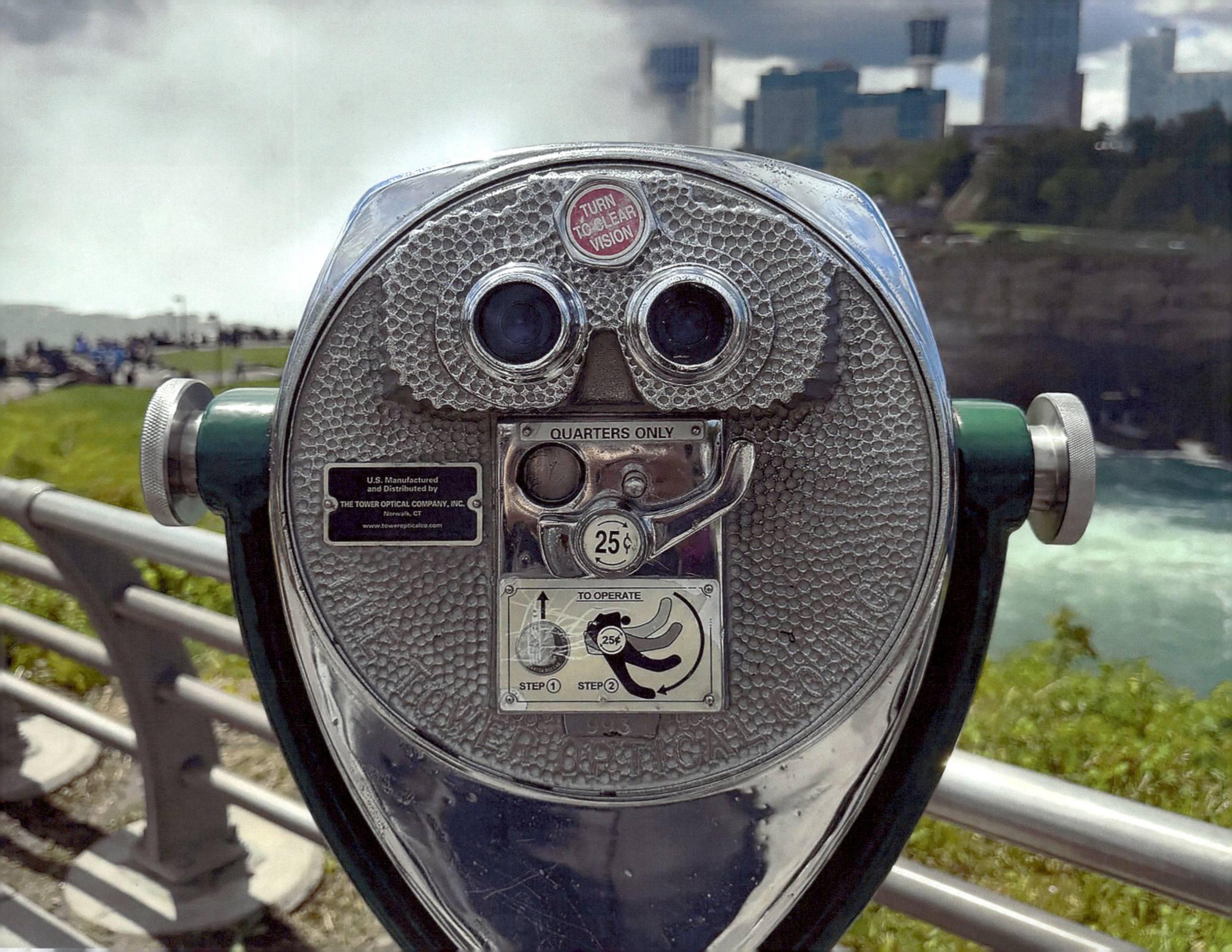

A closer look at the power and wonder of Niagara Falls

Our Wonders Never Cease

With a thunderous roar, Niagara Falls plunges into the gorge below, sending up a misty cloud scattered with rainbows—a breathtaking spectacle that leaves an indelible impression. It's no surprise that this awe-inspiring site is considered one of the natural wonders of the world, drawing more than 20 million visitors annually from across the globe.

A symbol of the American and Canadian landscapes, Niagara Falls is renowned for its dramatic waterfalls, swirling rapids, and sweeping vistas. Straddling the border between Ontario, Canada, and New York, USA, it stands as one of the most iconic and must-see destinations for lovers of nature and adventure alike.

Niagara Falls consists of three distinct waterfalls: the impressive Horseshoe Falls, the stately American Falls, and the delicate Bridal Veil Falls. Horseshoe Falls, the largest and most powerful, boasts the highest flow rate of any waterfall and over 3,160 tons of water pouring over the crest each second, its thunderous presence can be seen, heard, and felt from miles away.

But the wonder of Niagara Falls goes beyond its sheer power. Set along the ancient Niagara Escarpment—sculpted over millennia by glaciers and the Great Lakes—the falls are a geological treasure. They also play a vital role in energy production, generating more than 4 million kilowatts of electricity for communities on both sides of the border.

Niagara Falls is more than a natural marvel—it's a place rich in history, romance, and adventure. From exhilarating boat tours that bring you face to face with the mighty cascades to mesmerizing nighttime light shows, every experience here is unforgettable.

Whether you're hoping to capture stunning photos, feel the mist against your skin, or simply witness nature at its most powerful, Niagara Falls offers an unmatched journey. Come and see for yourself why it continues to inspire wonder in travelers from around the world.

Discover the Wonder of Niagara Falls

When people hear "Niagara Falls," they often picture one massive waterfall. But surprise—there are actually three! The American Falls and the delicate Bridal Veil Falls are on the U.S. side, while the dramatic Horseshoe Falls sits mostly in Canada. The best part? You can experience all three from the American side!

Niagara Falls was born over 12,000 years ago at the end of the last Ice Age, carved out by the same glacial forces that created the Great Lakes. It might sound ancient, but in nature's timeline, it's just a blink!

This iconic destination also happens to be America's oldest state park. We owe its preservation to a group of passionate environmentalists, including famed landscape architect Frederick Law Olmsted (the mastermind behind New York City's Central Park). Concerned about growing commercial development, they pushed for New York State to protect the area. Thanks to their efforts, Niagara Falls State Park was established in 1885.

While Niagara's vertical drop is an impressive 176 feet, it's not the tallest in the U.S.—that title goes to Yosemite Falls, standing at 2,425 feet. But what Niagara lacks in height, it more than makes up for in sheer power and size: over 700,000 gallons of water per second thunder over the edge at around 25 mph. It's the largest waterfall in North America by volume and width!

The Falls are part of the world's largest freshwater system—water from Lakes Superior, Michigan, Huron, and Erie flows into the Niagara River, then over the Falls, before heading into Lake Ontario.

Niagara Falls isn't just a natural wonder—it's also a marvel of science and innovation. Back in 1885, Nikola Tesla and George Westinghouse built the world's first hydroelectric power plant here. Today, Niagara generates about 4 million kilowatts of electricity—enough to power over a quarter of New York State and parts of Ontario!

Each year, more than 8 million visitors from around the world come to witness the magic of Niagara Falls. And yes—fish do go over the Falls! Most survive the plunge by going with the flow, though they might be a little dazed (and dodging hungry seagulls) afterward.

Over thousands of years, the Falls have gradually eroded—originally located about 7 miles down-stream near today's Lewiston. Thanks to modern water management, erosion has slowed to about 1 foot per year, and in the future, it could be as little as 1 foot every 10 years. Still, in tens of thousands of years, the Falls may eventually vanish into Lake Erie.

So whether you're here for the breathtaking views, the history, the adventure, or just the roar of the water, one thing's for sure: Niagara Falls is truly unforgettable.

Great Lakes Garden

Welcome Center

Green Island

Goat Island

Three Sisters Islands

Prospect Point

servation Tower

id of Mist

American Falls

Luna Island

Bridal Veil Falls

Cave of the Winds

Parking

Top of the Falls Restaurant

Terripin Point

Maid of the Mist

Horseshoe/ Canadian Falls

Niagara Falls State Park

America's Oldest State Park | Est. 1885

Niagara Falls State Park is the oldest state park in the U.S. Established in 1885 as the Niagara Reservation, it was the first of several such reservations that eventually became the cornerstones to the New York State Office of Parks, Recreation and Historic Preservation.

Frederick Law Olmsted was a visionary for Niagara Falls State Park. He also designed Central Park in New York City.

Niagara Falls State Park stretches over 400 acres, with close to 140 acres of that underwater.

Green Island, situated between Goat Island and the mainland, was named after Andrew Green, first president of the commission at the State Reservation at Niagara. He was a very prominent professional in New York City and was critical to the construction of Central Park, as well as the planning of northern Manhattan and today's Bronx. Green helped establish influential cultural institutions, such as the Museum of Natural History®, Metropolitan Museum of Art® and the Bronx Zoo®. Most importantly, he led the Greater New York movement that joined the municipalities around Manhattan Island into today's five-borough city.

Three Sisters Islands were named after the daughters of Parkhurst Whitney, a hotelman and prominent local citizen. The girls were named Asenath, Angeline and Celinda Eliza.

A statue of Chief Clinton Rickard, who was the founder of the Indian Defense League in 1926, can be found in the Welcome Plaza at Prospect Park.

An astounding 3,160 tons of water flows over Niagara Falls every second. This accounts for 75,750 gallons of water per second over the American and Bridal Veil Falls and 681,750 gallons per second over the Horseshoe Falls.

Water plunges at 32 feet per second over the Falls, hitting the base with 280 tons of force at the American and Bridal Veil Falls and 2,509 tons of force at the Horseshoe Falls.

Niagara Falls is capable of producing over 4 million kilowatts of electricity, which is shared by the United States and Canada.

Four of the five Great Lakes (Superior, Michigan, Huron

and Erie) drain into the Niagara River before emptying into Lake Ontario. These five Great Lakes make up almost one-fifth of the world's fresh water supply.

In November 1896, electrical power was transmitted from the Adams Power Plant in Niagara Falls to Buffalo. This was the first time in history that alternating current was transmitted over a long distance.

In 1969, an earthen dam was built across the head of the American Rapids, and the American Falls went dry. For six months, geologists and engineers studied the rock face and the effects of erosion. It was determined that it would be too costly to remove rock at the base of the American Falls, and that nature should take its course.

Over 12,000 years ago, Niagara Falls extended seven miles down river to what is now Lewiston, New York and Queenston, Ontario. Over the years, the brink has eroded, sometimes as much as six feet per year, to its present site.

Starting about 1.7 million years ago during the last Ice Age, continental glaciers up to two miles thick covered the Niagara Frontier region.

The first European to see and describe Niagara Falls in depth was Father Louis Hennepin, a French priest who accompanied LaSalle on his expedition to the Niagara region in 1678.

At one time, before Goat Island became part of Niagara Falls State Park, there were suggestions on what the island could be used for. W.K. Vanderbilt planned to use the island as a pleasure ground for people riding his trains to the Falls. P.T. Barnum wanted to turn Goat Island into circus grounds!

In 1885, a horse-drawn carriage ride around the Falls cost $1 per hour.

On January 27, 1938, the Upper Steel Arch Bridge, known locally as the Honeymoon Bridge, collapsed under pressure from the buildup of ice in the gorge below the Falls. The bridge had been closed days before in anticipation of the collapse.

On May 30, 2019 at 8:20 am, pro golfer Maurice Allen became the first person to hit a golf ball across the Horseshoe Falls. The ball was hit from Table Rock on the Canadian side of the Falls over to Terrapin Point on Goat Island spanning a distance of 393 yards through the mist and into a headwind. It landed on the sidewalk and finally came to rest in the grass, 427 yards from its takeoff point. This feat had previously been unsuccessfully attempted by John Daly in 2005.

Audubon designated the Niagara River Corridor as an Important Bird Area (IBA) in 1996, the first internationally-recognized area in the world. The river supports thousands of wintering gull and waterfowl species.

The lower Niagara River supports one of New York State's endangered fish, the lake sturgeon.

The Niagara River ecosystems support many of New York State's protected animal species. This includes the lake sturgeon, along with the peregrine falcon and American bald eagle.

The Niagara River Gorge is home to 14 species of rare plants, some threatened and endangered.

In 1901, 140 of the 170 trees native to Western New York were found growing on Goat Island.

The total number of flora species documented on Goat Island over the last two centuries is just over 600.

According to local legend, there were no black squirrels in Niagara Falls in the early 1800s, but there were in Canada across the river. When the first suspension bridge was built across the Niagara River, the avenue was open and the black squirrels crossed the river to the United States. We may never know if the story is true, but you can certainly catch a glimpse of this elusive critter in Niagara Falls today if you keep a sharp lookout!

The Birth of Niagara Falls as a Destination

Long before European explorers arrived, Native Americans living in the Niagara region were the first to witness the raw power and beauty of Niagara Falls. The first European to document the falls was French priest Father Louis Hennepin, who visited the area during a 1678 expedition. Overwhelmed by the magnitude of the waterfall, Hennepin later published A New Discovery, a travelogue that introduced Niagara Falls to the western world and sparked widespread interest in the region.

As the 1800s brought the expansion of the railroad, Niagara Falls became more accessible to travelers and quickly grew into a major tourist destination. One notable visitor was Jerome Bonaparte, younger brother of Napoleon, who honeymooned there with his American bride in 1804. This event is credited with beginning Niagara Falls' long-standing reputation as a honeymoon capital.

The Rise of Iconic Attractions

Niagara Falls' most famous attractions date back centuries. The Cave of the Winds originated in the 19th century when a rock overhang allowed adventurous visitors to stand beneath the falls. In its earliest days, daredevils descended by rope; eventually, staircases—and later, elevators in 1925—made the experience more accessible. Today, the Cave of the Winds, located on Goat Island in Niagara Falls State Park, allows visitors to walk a network of wooden decks to within 25 feet of Bridal Veil and Luna Falls, including the wind-whipped "Hurricane Deck."

Another enduring attraction is the Maid of the Mist, which dates back to 1846. Originally launched as a border-crossing ferry, it became a sightseeing vessel after the construction of the first international bridge made the ferry obsolete. The second vessel, Maid of the Mist II, was launched in 1854. Today, the attraction continues with all-electric boats named Tesla, honoring Nikola Tesla's pivotal role in harnessing the power of the falls.

Industry Meets Nature

Niagara's immense power also attracted industrialists. In 1895, the world's first large-scale hydroelectric power station was built nearby, though early systems using direct current (DC) could transmit electricity only short distances. That changed in 1896, when Nikola Tesla developed the alternating current (AC) induction motor, allowing electricity to travel farther—ushering

in a new era of power distribution that still powers the world today.

However, industrial development took its toll on the natural landscape. Concerned by this exploitation, renowned landscape architect Frederick Law Olmsted—famous for designing New York's Central Park—led efforts to protect the American side of Niagara Falls. His advocacy resulted in the 1885 Niagara Appropriations Bill, establishing Niagara Falls State Park—the first state park in the United States.

Olmsted envisioned a sanctuary where people could find renewal in nature. His legacy continues today, as visitors stroll peaceful paths on Goat Island, pass through native vegetation, and enjoy breathtaking views from Three Sisters Island and Terrapin Point, where Horseshoe Falls roars in the distance.

A Timeless Wonder

Each year, over 8 million visitors are drawn to Niagara Falls. While modern attractions and electric boats define today's experience, the awe-inspiring natural wonder and rich history continue to captivate, just as they did for the Native Americans, early explorers, honeymooners, and adventurers who came before.

ICE BRIDGE, NIAGARA 1912

2358-16

A Year-Round Wonder

Anytime Is the Right Time

No matter when you visit, Niagara Falls offers an unforgettable experience. Whether you're chasing springtime blossoms, summer thrills, autumn colors, or winter serenity, this natural wonder delivers in every season. Consider what kind of trip you're looking for—vibrant and social, peaceful and scenic, or adventurous and unique—and let the seasons guide your perfect Niagara Falls getaway.

Niagara Falls is one of the world's most iconic natural wonders—and it offers a completely different experience depending on when you visit. From the lush blooms of spring to the icy beauty of winter, each season brings its own magic to this must-see destination. Wondering when to plan your trip? Here's what you can expect throughout the year:

Spring Nature's Reawakening (March to May)

As winter fades, Niagara Falls bursts back to life. Melting snow and ice fuel the falls to their most powerful flow, creating dramatic mist and thunderous roars. The landscape comes alive with budding trees and blooming flowers, adding color and energy to every view.

Summer : Peak Season Fun (June to August)

This is the most popular time to visit—and for good reason. With warm weather, long sunny days, and a festive atmosphere, summer at Niagara Falls is full of life. Outdoor attractions are in full swing, and the area buzzes with energy.

Autumn: A Colorful Escape

(September to November)

As the air turns crisp, the surrounding landscape transforms into a canvas of fiery reds, oranges, and golds. Fall at Niagara Falls is a breathtakingly beautiful time to visit, with fewer crowds and mild weather making it ideal for a relaxing getaway.

Winter: A Frozen Wonderland

(December to February)

Don't let the chill stop you—winter is a magical time to see Niagara Falls like never before. The partially frozen falls create dazzling ice formations, and the mist turns trees and railings into glittering sculptures. It's like stepping into a snow globe. While the falls have never completely frozen, they've come close! Ice can create the illusion of a frozen waterfall—truly a sight to behold.

American Falls

Get ready to be awed by one of nature's most powerful spectacles—the American Falls, one of three stunning waterfalls that make up Niagara Falls.

The American Falls is the second largest of the three waterfalls that collectively form Niagara Falls along the Niagara River, straddling the Canada–United States border. Unlike the much larger Horseshoe Falls— approximately 90% of which lies in Ontario, Canada, and 10% in New York State—the American Falls is located entirely within the United States.

The American Falls receives about 11% of the Niagara River's flow, while the majority cascades over Horseshoe Falls. Goat Island separates the two. The crest of the American Falls is roughly 830 feet (250 meters) wide in a straight line, extending to about 950 feet when measured along its uneven edge. The water flowing over the crest is approximately 2 feet deep.

The height of the falls ranges between 70 and 110 feet from the top to the rock pile (talus) at the base. From the top of the falls to the river below, the total height measures 188 feet.

Visitors can view the American Falls from various vantage points on the U.S. side, including close-up views near the edge. Excellent views are available from the riverbank, as well as from Goat Island and Luna Island, both accessible by pedestrian bridges over the upstream rapids. From the Canadian side in Niagara Falls, Ontario, the falls are visible head-on.

The ledge of the American Falls is shaped like a modified "W", a result of over 150 years of rockfalls that have created a large talus mound at its base. One of the most significant collapses occurred in 1954 with the fall of Prospect Point to the north.

In 1969, the U.S. Army Corps of Engineers temporarily stopped the flow over the American Falls from June to November to study erosion and evaluate how to preserve

the falls. While reports conflict about whether tourism increased or decreased during this period, many visitors came to witness the rare sight of a dry falls. Ultimately, in the mid-1970s, authorities decided against any major alterations, choosing instead to let natural processes continue.

Often referred to as the "American side" of Niagara Falls, the American Falls lies to the far left of Horseshoe Falls, between Prospect Point and Luna Island, entirely within New York State. It is illuminated nightly in multiple colors, creating a striking visual display.

Despite being taller than Horseshoe Falls, no daredevils have attempted stunts over the American Falls. The Horseshoe Falls is favored for such feats due to its higher water volume and curved shape.

Facts About the American Falls

Height: 180 feet

Crestline Width: 1,075 feet

Estimated Water Flow: 75,000 gallons per second

Notable Rockfall: 1954 collapse near Prospect Point

Ongoing erosion, driven by the high water flow and the falls' composition of soft shale and limestone, suggests that the American Falls may eventually evolve into a series of rapids.

Ralph C. Wilson Welcome Center

The newly redesigned Ralph C. Wilson, Jr. Welcome Center at Niagara Falls State Park offers a blend of indoor and outdoor spaces, delicious dining options, and a rich dive into the area's storied past.

Spanning 28,000 square feet, the center features striking glass walls and a low-profile roof to frame stunning views of the Falls. It includes modern ticketing and information desks, expanded concession areas, updated restrooms, and essential support spaces. Thoughtful design touches like a rooftop solar array, bird-safe patterned glass, green roof elements, and an additional stand-alone restroom building enhance the visitor experience. The surrounding grounds also boast accessible paths, native plantings, and clear wayfinding elements for seamless exploration.

The project's final phase will introduce immersive museum spaces, bringing the region's natural, industrial, and Indigenous American history to life through interactive exhibits and outdoor displays.

Thanks to an $8 million contribution from the Ralph C. Wilson, Jr. Foundation, the center proudly bears the name of the late Buffalo Bills owner and American Football League co-founder, honoring his enduring legacy.

Niagara Falls State Park Observation Tower

The Niagara Falls State Park Observation Tower offers the only panoramic view of all three majestic waterfalls that make up Niagara Falls: the American Falls, Bridal Veil Falls, and Horseshoe Falls. Standing 282 feet (86 meters) tall, this striking structure, made from aluminum, glass, and steel, rises from the bottom of the gorge, accessible via ground-level entry from the park.

Visitors can take high-speed elevators to the base of the gorge, where they can board the iconic Maid of the Mist boat tour or ascend the nearby stairs to the Crow's Nest for a closer, multi-sensory encounter with the American Falls, complete with the cooling spray of mist.

The tower is also a haven for bird enthusiasts, offering a prime vantage point for spotting peregrine falcons, bald eagles, and a variety of gull species. The Niagara Gorge itself has been designated an Audubon Important Bird Area

ACE TO MAID OF THE MIST
OBSERVATION DECK

ETS

Ticket Price
Adult

RESTꞰOꞰS

(IBA), making it a popular site for wildlife observation.

Originally constructed in 1961, the tower underwent extensive renovations from 2001 to 2003, which included the addition of a pre-cast concrete observation deck, a sleek stainless steel railing system, upgraded elevators, new restrooms, and a gift shop.

This historic site, once part of the High Bank Industrial/Mill District, now draws over eight million visitors annually, who come to marvel at the falls by day and experience their vibrant, illuminated beauty by night – a spectacle often capped by breathtaking fireworks.

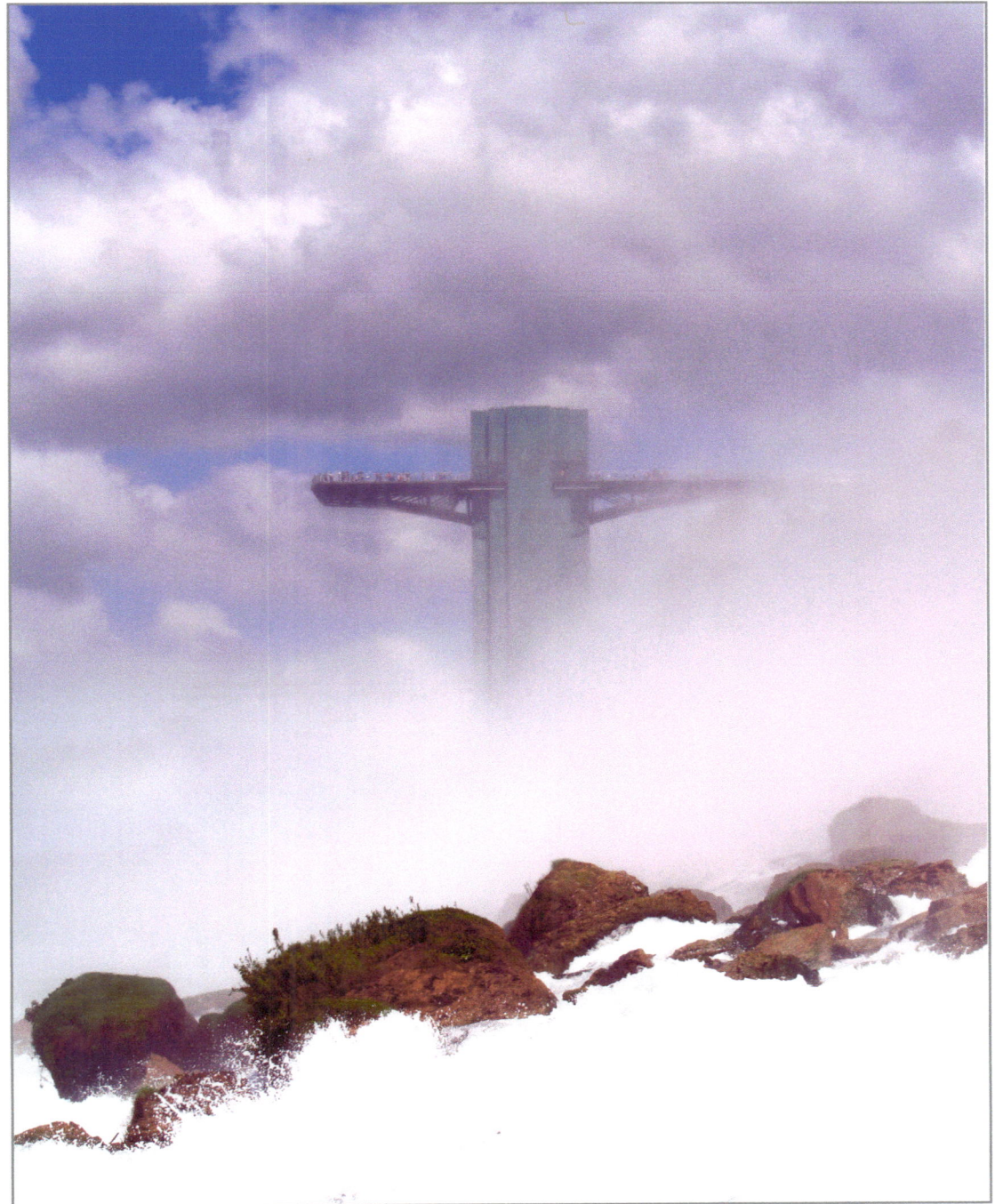

Maid of the Mist

The Maid of the Mist is a world-famous sightseeing boat tour that has been thrilling visitors to Niagara Falls since 1846. Departing from the American side in Niagara Falls, New York, the tour briefly crosses into Canadian waters, offering passengers a close-up view of the thundering cascades. The tour is operated by the Maid of the Mist Corporation, a family-owned business led by Chairman and CEO James V. Glynn, who joined the company as a ticket seller in 1950 before purchasing it in 1971.

Origins and Early Days:

The original Maid of the Mist was built in 1846 as a 72-foot-long, side-wheeled steamer designed to ferry passengers between New York City and Toronto. Powered by a wood and coal-fired boiler, it carried up to 100 passengers. However, the completion of a suspension bridge over the Niagara River in 1848 reduced the need for ferry services, prompting the owners to reinvent the boat as a sightseeing vessel, bringing tourists closer to the roaring waters of the Falls.

Growth and Modernization:

The current Maid of the Mist Corporation was formed in 1884 by Captain R. F. Carter and Frank LaBlond. They commissioned Alfred H. White of Ontario to build a new vessel, which launched in 1885. By the mid-20th century, steam-powered boats were phased out in favor of more powerful diesel vessels, with the first steel-hulled Maids launched in 1955 and 1956 by the Russel Brothers of Ontario. These ships could carry significantly more passengers, supporting the growing demand for the iconic tour.

Electrifying the Fleet:

In 2020, under the leadership of company president Christopher M. Glynn, the Maid of the Mist embraced a new era of sustainability, introducing two cutting-edge, fully electric vessels. Named James V. Glynn and Nikola Tesla, these boats are powered by lithium-ion batteries, reducing emissions while maintaining the thrilling, mist-soaked experience for passengers. The Tesla name-sake honors the pioneering electrical engineer whose work on alternating current (AC) power, patented and commercialized by George Westinghouse, helped harness Niagara Falls' immense energy.

Legacy and Cultural Significance:

The Maid of the Mist remains a powerful symbol of Niagara Falls' enduring appeal, blending natural wonder with human engineering. Its name is thought to reference the Iroquois myth of Lelawala, a story deeply rooted in the region's cultural heritage.

Crow's Nest

-The "Crow's Nest" is a staircase situated alongside the American Falls, offering visitors the chance to ascend halfway up the Falls for stunning, up-close views before descending back into the Gorge.

Tourists will soon have a chance to get even closer to Niagara Falls. Currently, visitors must return to the upper level via the Maid of the Mist elevators, creating significant pedestrian congestion during peak seasons.

Upon completion, this $9 million project will provide a much-needed alternative for accessing the Niagara Gorge, helping to ease foot traffic in the lower gorge. During the busy season, the stairs will serve as a one-way egress from the lower gorge, while in the off-season, they will offer two-way access to the overlook.

The project is being funded by State Parks capital funding, the Maid of the Mist Corporation, the Niagara River Greenway, and the federal Land and Water Conservation Fund. Work is expected to be completed in time for the 2026 season.

CAUTION
ROUGH
AND
SLIPPERY

Prospect Point

f you're visiting Niagara Falls, Prospect Point is one spot you don't want to miss. Located in Niagara Falls State Park, it's the best place in the U.S. to see the breathtaking American Falls up close. Before the water tumbles over the edge, the Niagara River drops about 50 feet over a half-mile stretch — a dramatic prelude to the powerful falls.

A Glimpse into the Past

Back in 1835, a wooden observation platform was built right here at Prospect Point. It stretched out over the gorge, supported by sturdy tree trunks. Though simple in design, it gave early visitors a thrilling view. The platform stood for ten years before being taken down in 1845 — not because of an accident, but as a precaution for safety.

The Great Rockfall of 1954

Fast forward to July 24, 1954, when nature made history. A massive chunk of Prospect Point collapsed — about 185,000 tons of rock fell into the Niagara Gorge below. It was the biggest rockfall here since 1931.

Experts quickly arrived to assess the danger. Two sections of the viewing area were still hanging over the edge, and another 50,000 tons of rock looked ready to fall. Officials debated whether blasting would be needed to stabilize the area.

Even diners at the nearby Rainbow Room Restaurant (in what is now The Brock Niagara Falls–Fallsview Hotel) had front-row seats to this natural drama, watching the deep hole left behind in the cliff face.

To protect visitors and workers, the Niagara Frontier State Parks Commission sprang into action. On August 6, they began controlled blasting to remove unstable rock, starting with 80 tons near the edge.

Then, on August 12, a powerful 95-pound dynamite blast brought down another 1,800 tons of rock. Around 400 people watched it happen. But one last blast was still needed.

A Special Moment

On August 16, 1954, a remarkable young girl made history. Debbie Stone, a 4-year-old from California who was paralyzed, was chosen to trigger the final dynamite blast — using her nose! Thanks to a special setup, her signal traveled across the country by telephone and set off the charge. 900 tons of rock crashed into the gorge, safely clearing the remaining danger.

Thanks to these efforts, Prospect Point has remained safe ever since, letting millions of visitors enjoy the incredible view without worry.

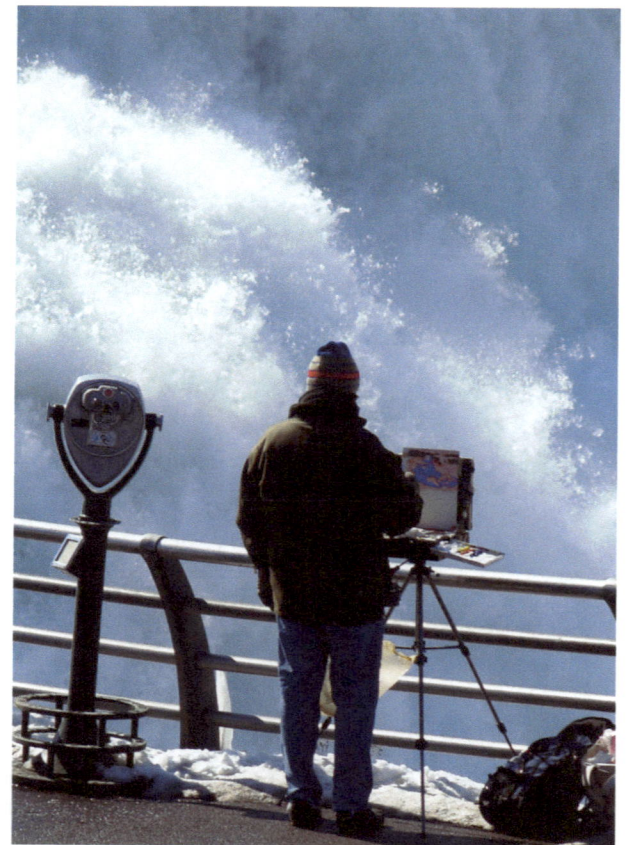

44

Niagara Falls Scenic Trolley

Experience the beauty of Niagara Falls State Park aboard the Niagara Scenic Trolley—a vintage-style, eco-friendly ride that lets you explore the park with ease. Operating exclusively within the state park, the trolley offers a convenient hop-on, hop-off service at popular attractions like Maid of the Mist, Cave of the Winds, and scenic viewpoints along the Falls.

This 3-mile guided route includes fun facts, historical insights, and helpful tips to make the most of your visit. Operating seasonally from May through October, the trolley pass is valid all day, so you can explore at your own pace.

See the Falls—Faster and Smarter

The Niagara Scenic Trolley offers a narrated overview of the park, sharing insider information and lesser-known details about its top attractions. Please note, due to high demand, trolleys often reach capacity. Wait times may vary, especially on weekends. For the best experience, arrive early or consider visiting on a weekday. Seating is not guaranteed; some passengers may be asked to stand, and large groups may need to split between cars. Always follow safety instructions from the driver and conductor.

An express shuttle is also available between Prospect Point and the Aquarium of Niagara/GL360, and can be boarded just north of Maid of the Mist.

Comfortable, Clean, and Green

Our trolleys run on eco-friendly natural gas, and are equipped with air conditioning in summer and heating in winter to keep you comfortable. As part of Niagara Falls State Park's Green Park Project, this service has earned the Clean Air Excellence Award for its commitment to environmental sustainability.

Accessible for All

The Niagara Scenic Trolley is ADA-compliant, making it easy for individuals with limited mobility to enjoy all that Niagara Falls State Park has to offer.

Goat Island

Today, Goat Island may be goat-free, but its name carries a legacy. In the late 1700s, early settler John Stedman kept a herd of goats here. After the brutal winter of 1780 claimed all but one of them, the island earned the name we still use today.

Goat Island sits between the American and Horseshoe Falls and offers some of the best views of Niagara Falls. You'll find scenic lookouts like Terrapin Point, lush wooded trails, and easy access to the famous Cave of the Winds tour. It's connected to the mainland by two bridges that carry pedestrians, cars, and even a trackless train, and to Luna Island by a charming footbridge.

A Natural Wonderland

In 1879, famed landscape architect Frederick Law Olmsted — known for designing Central Park — marveled at the island's untouched beauty. He called Goat Island one of the most naturally beautiful forests he'd seen in his travels across North America. He believed the constant mist from the falls created the perfect environment for native plants to thrive.

Thanks to early preservation efforts, much of that natural beauty remains today.

A Pioneer of Preservation

In the mid-1800s, Augustus Porter, a local business-man, recognized the long-term value of Goat Island as a natural attraction. He purchased the island, resisted pressures to develop it, and even allowed members of the Tuscarora Nation to live there and sell handcrafted goods to tourists. Porter also built the first toll bridge to the island in 1817. Though it was swept away by ice, a new one was built the following year and was praised as "one of the most singular pieces of engineering in the world" by British naval officer Basil Hall. The bridge, nearly 700 feet long, became the region's most traveled walkway.

In 1885, Goat Island became part of Niagara Falls State Park, the oldest state park in the United States — a testament to the commitment to protect this extraordinary place for future generations.

Luna Island

Luna Island, situated between the American Falls and Bridal Veil Falls, is one of the three waterfalls that form Niagara Falls. Located along the northern edge of Goat Island at the rim of the Niagara Gorge, Luna Island spans roughly three-quarters of an acre. Originally connected by a wooden bridge built in the 1800s, this bridge was replaced with a more durable structure in the 20th century.

Visitors to Luna Island can stand just a few feet from the roaring waters of both the American Falls and Bridal Veil Falls, enjoying close-up views accessible by a short walk across the island. The island's name is said to come from the phenomenon of "lunar rainbows," which can occasionally be seen when the moonlight hits the mist rising from the falls, creating a ghostly spectrum of colors. These moonbows were once a common sight on bright, moonlit nights, but the modern nightly illumination of the falls has made them a rare occurrence.

In 1954, the island was closed to the public due to concerns over the stability of the underlying bedrock, which had become dangerously unstable, raising fears of rockfall. It remained closed until 1972, when a significant stabilization effort, made possible by the temporary de-watering of the American Falls in 1969, allowed for critical anti-erosion work. This included removing loose rock and shoring up the island's foundations, making it safe for visitors once again.

50

Bridal Veil Falls

Bridal Veil Falls is the smallest of the three waterfalls that make up Niagara Falls, located on the American side in New York. It is separated from the larger American Falls by Luna Island and from the iconic Horseshoe Falls by Goat Island. With a crest 56 feet wide, the falls face northwest, dropping a total of 181 feet from a crest elevation of 508 feet.

The waterfall's name comes from its delicate, veil-like appearance, formed by the thin sheet of water cascading down the cliff. It begins with a 78-foot vertical drop before tumbling over talus boulders to the Maid of the Mist pool 103 feet below.

Historically, Bridal Veil Falls has also been known as Luna Falls and Iris Falls. The name "Luna Falls" originated from the striking lunar rainbows that once formed in its mist under the light of a full moon, a phenomenon best viewed from the nearby Luna Island. However, as industrialization and artificial lighting diminished this natural spectacle, the more poetic and romantic name "Bridal Veil" became the prevailing term.

Today, visitors can get up close to the base of Bridal Veil Falls through the Cave of the Winds attraction, while a pedestrian bridge connects Goat Island to Luna Island just upstream of the crest, providing breathtaking views of this often-overlooked gem of Niagara.

Cave of the Winds

Experience Niagara Falls like never before at the Cave of the Winds – a thrilling adventure that takes you right to the base of the thundering Bridal Veil Falls. This unforgettable journey begins with a 175-foot elevator descent into the breathtaking Niagara Gorge, where you step out onto a series of redwood walkways, just 20 feet from the roaring cascades.

A History Carved in Stone

The original Cave of the Winds was a natural cave hidden behind Bridal Veil Falls, discovered in 1834 and once known as Aeolus's Cave, after the Greek god of winds. This 130-foot high, 100-foot wide, and 30-foot deep wonder attracted daring visitors for nearly a century. However, in 1954, a massive rockfall and subsequent dynamiting permanently sealed the cave. Today, the attraction lives on, offering a dramatic, up-close encounter with the Falls.

Face the Power of the Falls

Once you reach the base, you'll don a bright yellow poncho and specially designed sandals – a must for the intense spray and powerful winds that can reach up to 68 mph. Follow your guide over the wooden walkways to the famous Hurricane Deck, where the torrents of Bridal Veil Falls crash down just a few feet away, drenching you in mist and awe. On a sunny day, you might even catch a rainbow dancing in the spray – a sight you'll never forget.

Whether you're a thrill-seeker or a nature lover, the Cave of the Winds offers a one-of-a-kind adventure that brings you closer to the heart of Niagara Falls. Don't miss the chance to feel the raw power and hear the thundering roar of this natural wonder.

Seasonal Adventure

The walkways and decks are removed each fall to prevent ice damage and are carefully rebuilt each spring by dedicated park crews, typically reopening in late May.

Accessible for All

For those with limited mobility, a special deck has been built 150 feet from the base of the Falls, ensuring that everyone can feel the power and beauty of Niagara.

The Falls at Night
Experience the Magic: Illumination of Niagara Falls

Every night, as the sun sets, Niagara Falls comes to life in a whole new way—glowing with vibrant colors that dance across the cascading waters. This dazzling display of light is a must-see for every visitor and has a rich history dating back over 160 years!

It all began in 1860, when 200 Bengal lights were used to light up the Falls in honor of the Prince of Wales' visit. On September 14th, both the American and Horseshoe Falls were illuminated for the very first time, creating an unforgettable spectacle for those in attendance.

Since then, the Falls have been lit for many special occasions—from Royal visits in the late 1800s to the 1901 Pan-American Exposition. In 1879, electricity made its debut at Niagara Falls with arc lights powered by a waterwheel, and by 1907, more advanced systems were using colored gels to cast stunning hues across the water.

The real turning point came in the 1920s when a group of passionate local businessmen—nicknamed "The Generators"—raised funds to install permanent lighting. Their efforts led to the formation of the Niagara Falls Illumination Board in 1925, which continues to manage and maintain the lighting to this day.

Over the years, the technology has evolved—from carbon arc lights to powerful Xenon spotlights. In 2016, a major $4 million upgrade introduced a state-of-the-art LED system. These modern lights are twice as bright, more energy-efficient, and capable of producing a wider range of vivid colors—creating the most brilliant illumination Niagara Falls has ever seen.

The lights are operated from a special control room, where technicians use color-coded switches to craft the perfect display. Panels of red, blue, green, and yellow slide in front of the lights, creating that iconic rainbow effect that visitors know and love.

What to Expect During Your Visit

Nightly Illumination: The Falls are lit up every evening of the year from three different locations on both sides of the border.

"Inspired by Nature" Light Show: Don't miss this special five-minute show that plays every hour on the half-hour. This mesmerizing display is inspired by natural wonders like sunrises, sunsets, rainbows, and even the northern lights.

Niagara Falls glow in the night is an unforgettable experience. The colors reflecting off the mist and water create a magical scene that's perfect for photos—or just taking it all in. It's a moment you'll never forget!

Horseshoe / Canadian Falls

Horseshoe Falls is the largest of the three waterfalls that make up Niagara Falls, which straddles the Canada–United States border along the Niagara River. Approximately 90% of the river's water—after accounting for diversions used for hydroelectric power—flows over Horseshoe Falls. The remaining 10% is split between the American Falls and the Bridal Veil Falls.

Horseshoe Falls, also known as the Canadian Falls, is situated between Terrapin Point on Goat Island in New York, USA, and Table Rock in Ontario, Canada. When the boundary between the U.S. and Canada was formalized in 1819 following the Treaty of Ghent, the northeastern tip of Horseshoe Falls lay within the United States, wrapping around the Terrapin Rocks, which were then connected to Goat Island by bridges.

In 1955, the space between the Terrapin Rocks and Goat Island was filled in, forming what is now Terrapin Point. In the early 1980s, the U.S. Army Corps of Engineers extended the land further by building diversion dams and retaining walls, redirecting water flow away from Terrapin Point. This effort resulted in the loss of about 400 feet (120 meters) of the original width of Horseshoe Falls. However, natural erosion continues to reshape the falls and may eventually impact the exact boundary between the two nations.

Today, official maps from both Canada and the United States show that a small portion of Horseshoe Falls still lies within U.S. territory.

Niagara Falls consists of three separate waterfalls: the Horseshoe Falls, the American Falls, and the Bridal Veil Falls. The Horseshoe Falls, located between Goat Island and Table Rock, are the most powerful and visually impressive of the three, drawing millions of tourists annually.

Historical studies reveal that thousands of years ago, Niagara Falls was located about 7 miles downstream from its current position. Over time, erosion—particularly on the Canadian side—caused the falls to retreat upstream at a rate of up to 1 meter per year until the early 1950s. Since then, managed water diversions have helped distribute the flow more evenly, significantly slowing the erosion rate.

In addition to its natural beauty, the Canadian Horseshoe Falls is a key source of hydropower generation. While there are over 500 waterfalls worldwide that are taller, Niagara Falls ranks among the largest by water volume, with an astounding average flow of 750,000 gallons per second.

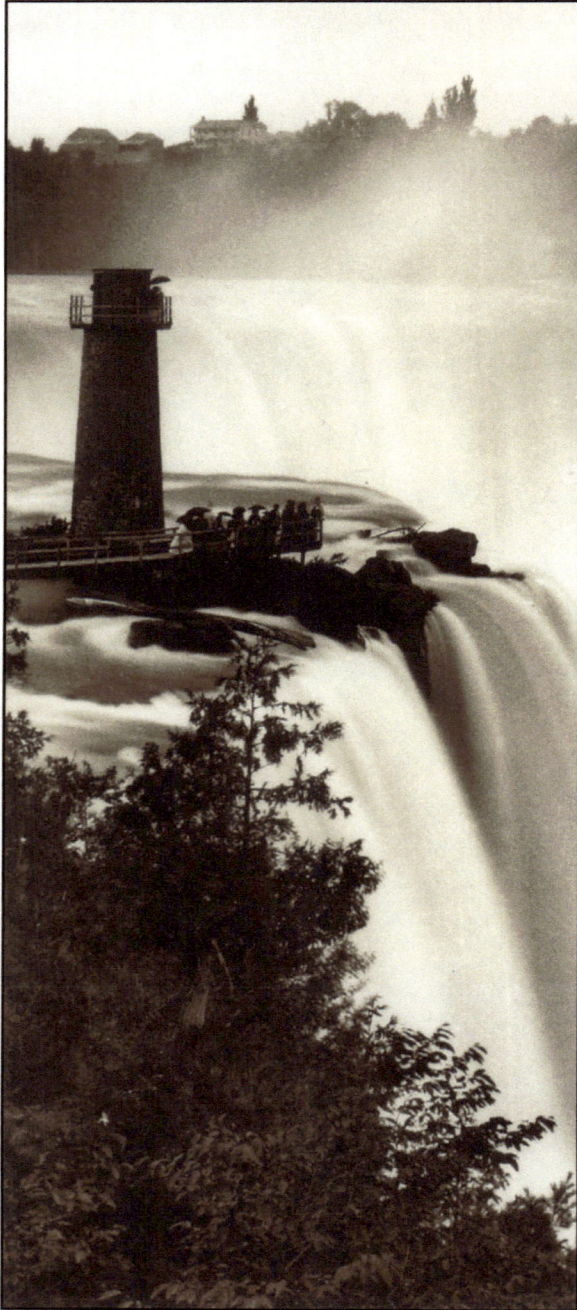

Terrapin Point:
Historic Viewpoint at the Edge of Niagara Falls

Terrapin Point, located at the western tip of Goat Island in Niagara Falls, New York, offers some of the most breathtaking views of the iconic Horseshoe Falls. Part of Niagara Falls State Park, this vantage point stands just steps from the thundering brink, making it one of the most immersive ways to experience the falls from the U.S. side.

A Storied Past

Originally known as Terrapin Rocks, this site was once a series of rock formations resembling giant turtles, perched right at the edge of the falls and separated from Goat Island. In 1827, brothers Peter and Augustus Porter—then owners of the land—constructed a 300-foot wooden bridge connecting Goat Island to these rocks. By 1833, they had added Terrapin Tower, a lighthouse-like structure rising between 30 and 45 feet high, offering early tourists a spiral climb to sweeping views of the falls *(Left)*. While popular, the tower was also criticized for detracting from the natural beauty and was demolished in 1873.

The original wooden bridge remained visible in photos up until the mid-20th century but eventually disappeared as the landscape evolved.

Transformation of the Landscape

In the mid-1950s, a major engineering effort reshaped the area. During a dredging project in 1954–1955 to redistribute the flow of the upper Niagara River more evenly over Horseshoe Falls, debris from the project was used to fill in the Terrapin Rocks area. This expansion created the Terrapin Point we know today and was officially turned over to the New York State Division of Parks on November 3, 1955.

Due to concerns about the stability of the site, Terrapin Point was closed in 1969. In 1983, the U.S. Army Corps of Engineers undertook a massive stabilization effort: 25,000 tons of unstable rock were removed, retaining walls and diversion dams were built, and additional landfill was added. These modifications eliminated approximately 400 feet of the Horseshoe Falls' crestline—about 100 feet of which extended into Canada. While some sources now claim the Horseshoe Falls lies entirely in Canada, others suggest that "most" of it does.

The site was reopened to visitors in September 1983 after extensive safety improvements and surface scaling.

Terrapin Point Today

Today, Terrapin Point is a well-maintained and easily accessible observation area, complete with paved paths and railings for safety. Open year-round, it provides a close-up encounter with one of nature's most awe-inspiring spectacles. Visitors often leave damp from the rising mist, especially in warmer months, as they take in panoramic views of the Horseshoe Falls, Bridal Veil Falls, and the powerful Niagara River.
Cultural and Historical Significance

Terrapin Point is believed to have been a sacred site for Native American tribes, who are said to have offered war trophies and personal items to the Great Spirit of Niagara from the nearby bluff, once known as Porter's Bluff.

In 1829, Terrapin Tower, built by General Parkhurst Whitney, became one of the earliest towers constructed at Niagara Falls. Though it was later destroyed in 1872—primarily to avoid competition with a proposed tower at Prospect Point (which was never built)—its memory lives on in the evolution of the site.

Even after the tower's demolition, a timber walkway remained for decades and was eventually replaced by a steel catwalk. In 1954, this walkway was removed, and the area was further modified to accommodate safer viewing and to manage water flow affected by upstream diversions for hydroelectric power.

A Place for the Bold

Terrapin Point also holds a unique place in modern history. On June 15, 2012, daredevil Nik Wallenda began his famous high-wire walk across Niagara Falls from Terrapin Point, making him the first person to cross directly over the falls in such a fashion.

Whether you're seeking a peaceful moment with nature, a place rich in history, or the perfect photo opportunity, Terrapin Point remains one of the most dramatic and accessible locations to experience the grandeur of Niagara Falls.

Three Sisters Islands:
Historic and Scenic Gem of Niagara Falls

Located just off the southern shoreline of Goat Island in Niagara Falls, New York, the Three Sisters Islands are a series of four small islands connected by pedestrian bridges. They offer visitors dramatic views of the Niagara River's rapids just before the water plunges over Horseshoe Falls.

These islands are steeped in both natural beauty and rich history. Long before European settlers arrived, the Iroquois people considered the islands sacred. Shamans would journey to them to offer gifts and commune with He-No, the Mighty Thunderer, believed to dwell in the misty cave at the base of the falls. Even today, some believe the spiritual energy of the place still lingers—modern psychics say you can hear the voices of spirits if you listen closely.

The islands are named after the three daughters of General Parkhurst Whitney—Asenath, Angeline, and Celinda Eliza—who were among the earliest visitors to the islands. In the spring of 1816, when ice jams in the river created a rare and temporary crossing, General Whitney took his daughters across the treacherous rapids on foot. Their daring journey reached the furthest island, previously inaccessible. Proud of their feat, Whitney persuaded the islands' owners, Peter and Augustus Porter, to name the islands in honor of his daughters. A fourth, smaller island nearby was later named Solon, after Whitney's infant son.

Originally known as the Moss Islands due to the rich moss covering their rocky surfaces, the islands feature a variety of microhabitats and plant life. Over time, the names of the islands became formalized: Asenath (nearest to Goat Island), Angeline (middle), Celinda Eliza (furthest), and Solon (also known as Little Brother Island).

The islands are accessible from Goat Island and are part of Niagara Falls State Park on the U.S. side of the border. A series of charming stone footbridges—built in the 19th century—connect the islands, allowing for peaceful strolls beneath leafy canopies, with up-close views of wildlife and the rushing river. This tranquil setting is ideal for reflection and nature appreciation, just steps away from one of the world's most powerful natural wonders.

Notably, in 1829, Francis Abbott, an Englishman enchanted by the area's natural beauty, chose to live as a hermit near the American Falls.

He often bathed in a cascade between Goat Island and Asenath Island—now known as Hermit's Cascade *(Opposite)* in his memory.

Over the years, the islands have changed slightly in size due to water diversion for hydroelectric power, but they remain a treasured destination. Whether for their spiritual history, botanical diversity, or breathtaking views, the Three Sisters Islands continue to be one of Niagara Falls' most enchanting and storied sites.

A Journey Through Time

Long before European settlers arrived, the land surrounding Niagara Falls was home to the Neutral Nation—an Indigenous people who lived peacefully between the Huron and Iroquois confederacies. The first recorded European to explore the region was French explorer Robert de La Salle. Accompanying him was Father Louis Hennepin, a Belgian priest who became the first European to document the grandeur of the falls. Scientists and artists followed: Pehr Kalm provided the first scientific account, and Captain Thomas Davies painted the earliest known visual depiction in 1762.

From Settlement to City

The City of Niagara Falls was officially incorporated on March 17, 1892, through the merger of the villages of Manchester and Suspension Bridge. Fittingly, the bill was signed into law on St. Patrick's Day, thanks in large part to Irish-American legislator Thomas Vincent Welch.

In the late 19th century, the city emerged as an industrial force. The powerful current of the Niagara River fueled factories that produced a wide range of goods, from abrasives to petrochemicals. While tourism was still in its infancy, the 20th century would see it rise to global prominence. By the 1920s, both industry and tourism were thriving. Immigrants flocked to the city to work in its bustling plants, while visitors came in droves to witness the thunderous spectacle of the falls. In 1927, the city expanded further by annexing the village of La Salle—named after the explorer himself.

Power and Progress

In 1956, tragedy struck when a portion of the Niagara Gorge wall collapsed, destroying the Schoellkopf Power Station. This disaster prompted the construction of a major hydroelectric facility in nearby Lewiston, overseen by planner Robert Moses. The project not only powered New York City but also brought a surge of new residents to the region.

Romance, Resistance, and Remarkable Stories

Niagara Falls quickly gained fame as a romantic destination. In 1801, Theodosia Burr Alston, daughter of U.S. Vice President Aaron Burr, honeymooned here. So did Napoleon's brother, Jérôme Bonaparte. By the mid-1800s, the falls had earned the nickname "Honeymoon Capital of the World."

But romance isn't the only legacy here. Niagara Falls played a critical role in the Underground Railroad. Its location on the U.S.–Canada border made it a key crossing point for enslaved people seeking freedom. Some succeeded with help; others faced peril. This legacy is preserved today at the Niagara Falls Underground Railroad Heritage Center.

Even Frederick Douglass was moved by the power of the falls, writing: "When I came into its awful presence, the power of description failed me."

(*Opposite:*) Niagara Falls by Father Louis Hennepin, 1698
This Belgian priest and adventurous missionary of the Recollet Order promoted the exploration of North America. Hennepin published three travel accounts (1683, 1697, and 1698) that were widely read in Europe. His work offered descriptions of landscapes, including the first of Niagara Falls which he describes as a "horrible precipice" and a "prodigious Cascade of Water … the Universe does not afford its Parallel."

Spectacle and Survival

Niagara has long been a place of awe and drama. In 1840, chemist Hugh Lee Pattinson captured one of the earliest photographs of the falls using a daguerreotype. In 1918, an iron barge known as the "iron scow" became lodged above the falls, where it still rests today. And in the winter of 1912, the American Falls froze solid, forming a giant natural sculpture that amazed onlookers.

That same year, the "ice bridge"—a temporary formation allowing people to cross the river—collapsed while visitors were on it, resulting in the tragic Ice Bridge Disaster.

Shaping and Protecting a Natural Wonder

Major modifications to the landscape came in the mid-20th century. Parts of Terrapin Point, near Goat Island, were filled in during the 1950s and again in the 1980s, shifting much of the Horseshoe Falls to the Canadian side of the border. While modern shipping bypassed the falls, they remained vital for clean, renewable hydroelectric power and continued to draw millions of tourists.

Before preservation efforts began, the land around the falls was largely in private hands, limiting public access. In the 1860s, famed landscape architect Frederick Law Olmsted began advocating for public ownership. Commissioned by the New York State Legislature, Olmsted and State Surveyor James T. Gardner published a landmark report in 1879 calling for the protection and public enjoyment of the falls.

(Left: The Niagara Movement, the immediate predecessor of the NAACP was a civil rights organization founded in 1905 by a group of activists—many of whom were among the vanguard of African-American lawyers in the United States—led by W. E. B. Du Bois and William Monroe Trotter. The group did not meet in Niagara Falls, but planned its first conference for nearby Buffalo July 9, 1905.)

To his Excellency Lieut.t Gen.l Sir Jeffrey Amherst, Knight of the Most Honourable Order of the Bath. &c. &c. &c.
These Six Views are most humbly Inscribed, by His Excellency's most devoted Serv.t Tho.s Davies.
An East View of the Great Cataract of Niagara.

J.Fougeron sculp.

Perpend.l Height of the Fall 162 Feet. Breadth about a Mile & Quarter.   Drawn on the Spot by Tho.s Davies Capt.t Lieut.t in the Royal Reg.t of Artillery.

An East View of the Great Cataract of Niagara, 1760 - Captain Thomas Davies. This is the earliest known visual depiction of Niagara Falls.

Schoellkopf Power Station

Their campaign, bolstered by the Niagara Falls Association formed in 1883, culminated in the passage of legislation signed by Governor Grover Cleveland that same year. This act led to the establishment of the Niagara Reservation in 1885—the first state park in the U.S. created through eminent domain. Olmsted and architect Calvert Vaux completed the park's design in 1887, emphasizing public access and natural beauty while resisting commercial development. The park became a National Historic Landmark in 1963 and remains a central part of the Niagara Falls National Heritage Area.

Niagara Falls Today

Today, Niagara Falls stands at the crossroads of nature, history, innovation, and romance. It continues to captivate visitors with its thundering waters, scenic vistas, and powerful stories—from ancient Indigenous heritage and heroic escapes to honeymoon traditions and renewable energy breakthroughs.

Niagara Falls State Park, widely considered the oldest continuously operating state park in the U.S., underwent a major $44 million restoration completed in 2003. Its upgraded observation tower, visitor center, and trails ensure that millions of visitors each year can experience this wonder safely and meaningfully.

In 2007, the park was named one of the "10 Most Beautiful Places in America"—a fitting tribute to a place where the past flows powerfully into the present.

(Above:) By the 1880s, the ice bridge had become a playground for the local population as well as tourists.

Daredevils

Over the Falls: Daring Feats and Unbelievable Stunts

Niagara Falls has long drawn thrill-seekers, daring souls willing to risk it all for a shot at immortality. It started in 1827, when local hotel freighter, loaded with live animals and human effigies, over the falls for a paying audience. The spectacle cost 50 cents a ticket and set the tone for a long tradition of audacious attempts.

The first real human daredevil appeared in 1829, when Sam Patch, known as "The Yankee Leapster," leaped from a high tower into the gorge and survived, igniting a century of stunts. By 1901, 63-year-old schoolteacher Annie Edson Taylor *(Below)* had become the first person to go over the falls in a barrel, emerging battered but alive. Upon exiting, she famously declared, "No one ought ever do that again." Of course, many would ignore her advice. She expected fame and fortune. Annie died in poverty.

Notable Moments in Falls History:

• Bobby Leach *(Opposite)* (1911) – Survived the plunge in a steel barrel but required rescue and suffered severe injuries. Bobby broke both kneecaps and his jaw during his daring event. Years later while touring in New Zealand, Bobby slipped on an orange peel and died from complications due to gangrene!
• Jean Lussier (1928) – Attempted the drop in a giant rubber ball and survived.

• On July 5th, 1930, 46-year-old George A. Stathakis, *(Left)* climbed in a massive 10-foot-long barrel made of wood and steel, bringing along his over 100 years old pet turtle, Sonny Boy, as a good luck charm.

The barrel survived the thunderous drop, but became trapped behind the rushing water for over 18 hours. Tragically, Stathakis didn't survive—he ran out of air before rescue crews could reach him. Miraculously, Sonny Boy the turtle lived through the ordeal

• Roger Woodward (1960) – Miraculously survived after being accidentally swept over the falls at age seven.

• Kirk Jones (2003) – Became the first known person to survive a plunge without any flotation device. Tragically, he died attempting a second descent in 2017.

Many of these daredevils faced fines, arrests, and life-threatening injuries. Today, attempts to go over the falls are illegal on both sides of the border, though that hasn't stopped the truly fearless from trying.

Walking the Sky: The Tightrope Legends

Before barrels and rubber balls, it was tightrope walkers who captivated Niagara's visitors. The first to cross the gorge was Jean François "Blondin" Gravelet *(Right)* in 1859. Known for his flair, he crossed the rope eight times that year, even carrying his manager on his back for one trip.

Maria Spelterini, a 23-year-old Italian, became the only woman to cross the gorge on a tightrope in 1876, performing stunts like blindfolded crossings or with her wrists and ankles shackled.

Most recently, in 2012, high-wire artist Nik Wallenda *(Opposite Page)* revived this tradition with a 550-meter (1,800-foot) crossing directly over the falls—a feat requiring special government approval and a passport for his landing on the Canadian side.

"It's Niagara Falls.
It's one of the most beautiful natural
wonders in the world.
Who wouldn't want to walk across it?"

— Nik Wallenda

90

The Honeymoon Capital of the World

For more than two centuries, Niagara Falls has held a special place in the hearts of newlyweds, earning its title as the "Honeymoon Capital of the World." This enduring association with romance traces its roots back to the early 19th century, when the falls became a favored destination for affluent couples seeking an unforgettable post-wedding journey.

The First Honeymooners: Theodosia and Joseph Alston (1801)

The tradition of honeymooning at Niagara Falls is often said to have begun in June 1801, when Theodosia Burr Alston and her husband, Joseph Alston, set out on a grand bridal tour from Albany, New York. Theodosia, the daughter of future U.S. Vice President Aaron Burr, and her husband traveled with a small entourage, including nine pack horses, to the remote and majestic falls. Their journey took them through the frontier settlement of Buffalo before arriving at the thundering cataracts, making them among the first known honeymooners to visit Niagara Falls.

Royal Influence and the Rise of a Tradition (1804)

Just a few years later, in 1804, another high-profile couple followed in their footsteps. Jerome Bonaparte, the younger brother of Napoleon, and his American bride, Elizabeth Patterson of Baltimore, made the long journey to Niagara. This high-society visit helped cement the falls' reputation as a fitting destination for newlyweds, adding a touch of European glamor to its allure.

Opening the Falls to the Masses

Initially, the arduous trip to Niagara Falls was reserved for the wealthy. However, the opening of the Erie Canal in 1825 made travel to the region much more accessible, transforming the falls into a must-see attraction for middle-class couples as well. This newfound accessibility sparked a surge in tourism, with the first large hotel on the Canadian side, the six-story Pavilion, opening in 1822. The American side soon followed, with establishments like the Eagle Hotel offering prime views of the roaring waters.

The Cultural Impact of the Falls

By the 1830s and 1840s, the idea of honeymooning at Niagara had taken firm root in the cultural imagination. Travel writings from the period make frequent references to young couples visiting the falls, and the 1841 song "My Niagara Falls Honeymoon" captured the spirit of this romantic pilgrimage. An 1839 newspaper even described seeing "several cooing couples near the Falls, both Canadian and American, fulfilling the fleeting period of their honey-lunacy."

Niagara in the Gilded Age and Beyond

By the mid-19th century, Niagara Falls had become a staple stop on the so-called "Northern Tour" for wealthy travelers. Southern aristocrats and European visitors alike flocked to the site during the summer months, drawn by both its natural splendor and its growing reputation as a place to see and be seen. This trend continued well into the 20th century, with the post-World War II tourism boom further solidifying Niagara's

The Lasting Legacy of Romance

Today, Niagara Falls continues to attract honeymooners from around the world, offering modern amenities alongside its timeless natural beauty. From the legendary Maid of the Mist boat tours to the dramatic views from the Skylon Tower, it remains a place where couples come to celebrate their love, just as they have for more than 200 years.

As the New York Times declared in 1935, "No other place in America attracts so many newly married couples as Niagara Falls." This reputation remains strong today, ensuring the falls' place in the hearts of lovers for generations to come. status as a honeymoon hotspot.

The 1953 film "Niagara" starring Marilyn Monroe again placed the falls in the national limelight. Marketing and tourism ads proclaim Niagara Falls to be the honeymoon capitol of the world, though Paris and several other locations vie for the title.

A Birdwatcher's Paradise

Niagara Falls USA isn't just a natural wonder for tourists — it's a haven for birds. Literally. The region attracts not only millions of visitors each year but also a stunning variety of bird species.

From soaring bald eagles and peregrine falcons to flocks of ducks, geese, and over 19 species of gulls, Niagara Falls, New York, offers exceptional birdwatching opportunities year-round. With scenic overlooks and rich natural habitats, it's no wonder this area is recognized as a globally significant Important Bird and Biodiversity Area (IBA).

Where to Watch

Birders can explore prime viewing spots like Niagara Falls State Park, the Niagara River, and Lake Ontario, where migratory routes, open water, and abundant food sources converge. Popular stake-out spots include the Observation Tower, Goat Island, and the Three Sisters Islands.

Fall & Winter

Though many birds migrate south in autumn, Niagara becomes a hotbed for birders during this time. Bonaparte's Gulls, Herring Gulls, and Ring-billed Gulls arrive in massive numbers — sometimes up to 30,000 Bonaparte's Gulls in one day, representing nearly 10% of the global population. These flocks are joined by a range of waterfowl, including canvasbacks, common mergansers, goldeneyes, greater scaup, and red-breasted mergansers.

Winter offers close views of ducks in their vibrant breeding plumage. Photographers and novice birders can easily spot common goldeneyes, bufflehead, long-tailed ducks, hooded mergansers, gadwalls, American wigeon, and even the striking harlequin duck near the falls.

Spring Migration

Late April through May is peak time for songbird migration. Birds returning from the southern U.S., Central and South America include swallows, sparrows, fly-catchers, herons, scarlet tanagers, rose-breasted grosbeaks, and vibrant warblers. Up to 30 warbler species can be spotted in May alone, making Niagara Falls a spring-time paradise for birdwatchers.

Terns are also abundant: common and Caspian terns are widespread, while Forster's and black terns appear during migration. The spring migration is also a great time to spot great egrets, pileated woodpeckers, and even the elusive and de-clining red-headed woodpecker.

Summer Sightings

Niagara Falls lies in the Carolinian ecoregion, home to species rarely seen further north. Birders can visit the Heronry above the falls on the Niagara River, where great egrets and black-crowned night herons feed their young. Look and listen for tufted titmice, Carolina wrens, fish crows, northern mockingbirds, and red-bellied woodpeckers, many of which are year-round residents.

Peregrine falcons, once endangered, have rebounded thanks to the banning of DDT. Watch them nest on cliff faces below Table Rock or skyscrapers around the falls, diving in spectacular hunting stoops. Bald eagles are also on the rise, with nesting pairs visible year-round and larger populations gathering in winter near Navy Island.

About The Author

Mark Donnelly, Ph.D. – Author & Photographer

Dr. Mark Donnelly is an accomplished author, artist, and educator. He is also a dedicated advocate for Western New York's waterfront, a proud husband, father of four remarkable adult children, a committed Mason, and a man rarely seen without his camera.

With 43 published books to his name, Dr. Donnelly has captured the spirit and beauty of Western New York in titles such as *The Fine Art of Capturing Buffalo, Frozen Assets, Statuesque Buffalo, There's So Much To Love, Shovel Ready City, Celebrating Buffalo's Waterfront*, and *A City Built by Giants*. His diverse body of work also includes children's literature and whimsical novelty cookbooks.

An award-winning photographer, Dr. Donnelly's imagery has been featured in numerous regional and national exhibitions. His work has appeared in prestigious venues such as the Albright-Knox Art Gallery, Burchfield Penney Art Center, Rodman Arts Centre, CEPA Gallery, The NACC, Big Orbit Gallery, Seattle Art Museum, ZGM Gallery, and the Art Gallery of Hamilton.

Thundering Niagara

Falling in love with the power and wonder of Niagara Falls, USA

Mark Donnelly, PhD & Friends

www.ingramcontent.com/pod-product-compliance
Lightning Source LLC
Chambersburg PA
CBHW040316270326
41926CB00004B/82